Edinburgh
AN OUTLANDER TOUR

Edinburgh
AN OUTLANDER TOUR

Ali Wood

TVTRAVELLER

Cover image: Street performer outside St Giles' Cathedral.
VisitScotland/Kenny Lam

Contents

Chapter 1: Introduction   **4**

Chapter 2: Old town walking tour   **14**

Map of Edinburgh   14
Scene-spotter   38

Chapter 3: Further afield   **97**

Now see Scotland   52
About the author   54

Chapter 1
Introduction

For Outlander fans, Edinburgh is a real treat. Not only is it packed with must-see film locations, but its real history provides much of the colour and inspiration for Diana Gabaldon's books. There's the fictional Jamie Fraser, of course, but there's also Bonnie Prince Charlie, the Jacobites and the Scottish Enlightenment... and Edinburgh is where it all comes together.

Scotland's capital is one of those rare cities that's absorbed modern architecture into its soul without changing a bit. From its 12th century castle and medieval wynds to its Georgian townhouses and modernist parliament, not a building feels out of place.

It's a beautiful city – much of it unchanged since Bonnie Prince Charlie rode across the cobbles, turning its female population into Jacobite supporters overnight.

Easily walkable, the heart of the city lies in the Royal Mile between the Palace of Holyroodhouse and Edinburgh Castle. Every day of the year it's living and breathing with circus performers, musicians, artists and traders. The aroma of street-food is as rich as the languages spoken, and bagpipes a constant backing track to the year-round stream of tourists.

Branching off like veins are the pulsating alleyways that climb or plummet to the next exciting street, flanked either side by townhouses barely an arm's width apart. Known as wynds – or closes if they're locked at night – they'll lure even the most map-abiding tourist astray.

So allow yourself two hours for a self-guided Outlander tour, then at least two days to get lost. If you come in August – during the festivals (Fringe, Art, Literature, International and Tattoo) – you'd better make that a week!

This tour weaves together film and book locations with historical facts. Now it's time to step back into Jacobite Scotland, gather your wits about you, and experience Edinburgh through the eyes of Jamie and Claire.

BEFORE OUTLANDER... THE HISTORY

The city of Edinburgh has been occupied since before history was written, with Iron Age hillforts still visible on Arthur's Seat – a striking peak that resides 822ft above the city.

In the 12th century, Edinburgh was established as one of Scotland's earliest royal burghs, protected by a fortress on the slope below Castle Rock. It remained largely in English hands, and became a major trading port, with hides and wool being routed through Leith. By the mid 14th century, French chronicler Froissart described it as 'the Paris of Scotland' with around 400 dwellings.

By 1560 – when the total population of Scotland reached a million, 12,000 of those were living inside Edinburgh, and a further 4,000 in separate jurisdictions such as Canongate and Leith. Despite outbreaks of plague, and high death rates linked with poor sanitary conditions and overcrowding, the population boomed.

Did you know?

Outlander character Geillis Duncan was named after a real woman who confessed to witchcraft after being tortured in the Old Tolbooth. Duncan was a 16th century maid, accused by her employer of having a miraculous healing ability and sneaking out of the house at night. She was also accused of conspiring to murder her godfather. Over a hundred suspected witches were arrested in the North Berwick Witch Trials in 1590, and many confessed under torture to meeting the Devil and attempting to sink the King's ship. If you confessed to being a witch in the 16th century, you'd be given the honour of being strangled before being burned on the stake at Castle Esplanade. The smell of burning flesh on the Royal Mile served as a warning to all. It was a brutal time, though Diana Gabaldon did some use artistic licence when it came to Geillis's trial: by the mid-1700s witches were no longer executed in Scotland.

MARY QUEEN OF SCOTS

Edinburgh, being mostly Protestant, was hostile to the six-year reign of Catholic Mary, Queen of Scots. She abdicated in 1567, and was briefly detained in the town provost's house (the present-day site of the Edinburgh City Chambers) before being sent to prison in Loch Leven Castle. Her 13-month-old son, James VI, became king, and was governed by four different regents until old enough to rule.

For the next 100 years, Edinburgh's town council was controlled by merchants, despite efforts by the kings' men to intervene. Social status and wealth mattered, but not religion.

In 1603 King James VI of Scotland succeeded to the English throne, uniting the monarchies of Scotland and England. However, Scotland remained a separate kingdom, retaining its parliament in Edinburgh. His son Charles I succeeded on his death in 1625 but was executed in 1649. Charles II was declared king in Edinburgh, but not England.

The following year, Edinburgh was occupied by Oliver Cromwell's forces. The Scottish Army tried to overturn Cromwell by invading England, but was defeated at the Battle of Worcester. It wasn't until 1660 that Charles II was restored to the throne. Known as the 'Merry Monarch', Charles ruled until his death in 1685 at which point his younger brother became king. Known in Scotland as King James VII and in England and

Mary with son James. In reality, she last saw him as a baby

Ireland as King James II, the Catholic ruler proved unpopular with the Protestant parliament. He fled to France in 1688, leaving the throne to his Protestant daughter Mary and her husband William of Orange.

THE BIRTH OF THE JACOBITES

James VII's son James Francis Edward rallied for the restoration of his father to the throne, and his supporters became known as Jacobites from 'Jacobus', the Latin version of James. The first major uprising took place in 1715, not just in Scotland, but Wales and Devon too. Whilst the southern rebellions were forestalled, the Scottish Jacobites fought their way into England before surrendering at the Battle of Preston.

After the 1715 rebellion most of lowland Scotland, like England, accepted the Hanoverian dynasty. However, the Highlanders continued to conspire for the restoration of the Stuart monarchy. In 1745 Prince Charles Edward Stuart, the 24-year-old son of James, tried to convince France to sponsor a second invasion. They declined, so the Young Pretender, as he was known in England, set off to Scotland to rally the Highland clans.

The prince landed in the Western Isles on 02 August and raised an army of 5,000 men. After several battles, the final encounter took place on Culloden Moor against the King's younger son, William, Duke of Cumberland. The Highlanders charged and were met by a hail of cannon and musket fire. Within half an hour 2,000 Jacobite men were dead and another 1,000 taken prisoner. Bonnie Prince Charlie escaped to France and the British dismantled the clan system, ending Jacobite support in the Highlands.

WHERE OUTLANDER COMES IN

In Outlander, Jamie's story begins in 1741 when he meets Captain Jack Randall for the first time. Two years later he meets Claire (who's time-travelled through the stones) and marries her. In 1745 he receives a letter from Charles Edward Stuart, who officially claims the throne. Claire and Jamie live in Edinburgh for a few months, where Jamie is a member of Charles Stuart's inner circle.

The Jacobite Rising is in full-swing, and Edinburgh is briefly occupied by the Jacobite Highland Army, before its march into England and eventual defeat at Culloden.

Fast-forward 20 years to Season 3 and the book Dragonfly in Amber. Jamie is once more living in Edinburgh, where he works as a printer with a smuggling business on the side. It's a prosperous city – a centre of medicine, law, science and engineering – but hugely overcrowded. Since the 12th century, Edinburgh's population has been enclosed within walls, and now the space between the Flodden and Telfer Walls is tight as ever. There are buildings 15 storeys high shared by families of all classes: the poor in the cellars, noblemen in the middle floors and shopkeepers in the attic.

The scholar Sir Gilbert Elliot describes Edinburgh as 'more crowded than in any other town in Europe' with 'upright streets'. It's during this time – the Scottish Enlightenment – that great minds meet, converging in homes, taverns and the streets, sparking ideas to keep the presses running day and night. This is why Jamie becomes a printer. It's 1766, Claire and Jamie are reunited, and your Outlander tour begins.

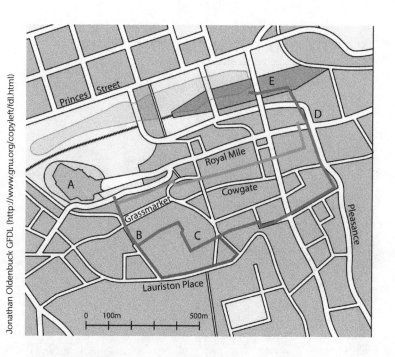

Jonathan Oldenbuck GFDL (http://www.gnu.org/copyleft/fdl.html)

Above is a map of central Edinburgh, showing the locations of the town walls, overlaid on the present day street pattern

KEY

- A: Edinburgh Castle
- B: Flodden Tower
- C: Greyfriars Kirkyard
- D: Netherbow Port
- E: Waverley station
- Orange line: King's Wall (c.1450-1475)
- Red line: Flodden Wall (c.1514-1560)
- Purple line: Telfer Wall (c.1620)
- Blue hatching shows extent of the former Nor Loch

MAP OF OLD TOWN WALKING TOUR

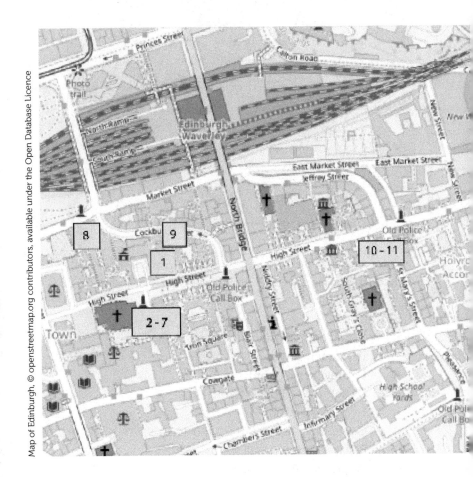

Map of Edinburgh. © openstreetmap.org contributors, available under the Open Database Licence

KEY

1: Mercat Cross
2: Parliament Square
3: Parliament Hall
4: Pissing Pony
5: Lothian Chambers
6: The Signet Library
7: The Old Tollbooth

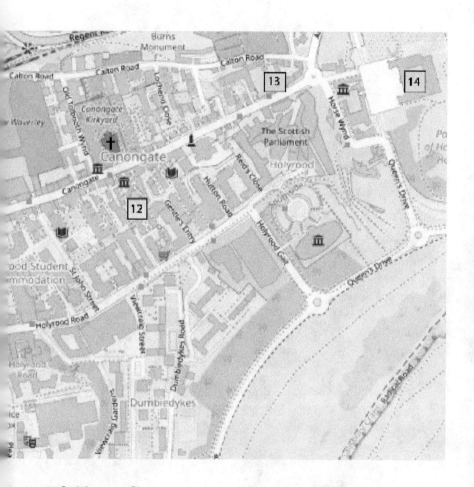

8: Advocate Close

9: Anchor Close

10: Tweeddale Court

11: The World's End Pub

12: Bakehouse Close

13: White Horse Close

14: The Palace of
    Holyroodhouse

Chapter 2
Old town walking tour

1. MERCAT CROSS, HIGH STREET

The market cross, or 'mercat cross' in Scotland was once a distinctive feature of almost every market town in Britain. It marks the square where the market's held, but more importantly is the centre of gossip, official proclamations and entertainment. In centuries gone by families would picnic at the cross and enjoy the day's entertainment – from music and acrobatics to shamings, torture and executions. Even today, Edinburgh's Mercat Cross is a hive of activity, with travellers waiting for tour guides, friends meeting up, and street artists performing tricks.

The Mercat Cross has been at the heart of civic life for centuries. It's here that important announcements were (and still are) made – from the end of World War II to the Queen's accession to the throne. On 18 September 1745 Bonnie Prince Charlie stood at the Mercat Cross and proclaimed his father King of Scotland, and himself Regent at the Cross. An elated crowd, many of them Jacobites, gathered to witness his proclamation, with the ladies waving white handkerchiefs in support of the exciting and dashing new prince.

A year later, following the prince's defeat at Culloden the captured Jacobite colours were ceremoniously burned.

In May 2018 the Mercat Cross was restored to its former

Left: The streets are alive during the Edinburgh Fringe

glory, and celebrated with a fanfare of the Queen's trumpeters and the singing of the National Anthem.

Though the current Mercat Cross is Victorian, there have been crosses in various guises at least since the 14th century. Any newcomer to the town would have made their way to Mercat Cross and found a caddie to carry their bags and show them to their lodgings. Though this doesn't happen in Outlander – Claire meets a boy on the Royal Mile – it's what a visitor in the 1700s would have done were they looking for the print shop of Alexander Malcolm.

• **Walk from Mercat Cross to Parliament Square**

2. PARLIAMENT SQUARE

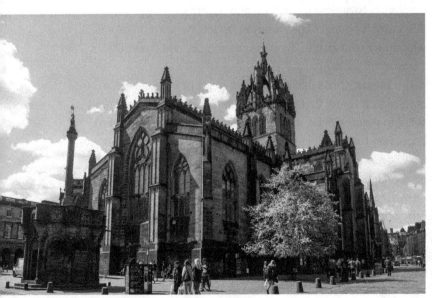

The Mercat Cross (left) and St Giles' Cathedral

VisitScotland/Kenny Lam

Just off the High Street is Parliament Square, which surrounds St Giles' Cathedral (also known as the High Kirk of Edinburgh) on three sides. The L-shaped area came into existence in 1632 as a forecourt to Parliament House. Before this time it was a graveyard to St Giles' Cathedral. At parking lot 23 Protestant reformer John Knox (1513 – 1572) is buried. Knox was the founder of the Presbyterian Church of Scotland, and called for the execution of Catholic Mary Queen of Scots.

3. PARLIAMENT HALL

The old parliament building played a crucial role in the relationship between Scotland and England, two independent kingdoms until the Acts of Union in 1707. It was here that Scotland elected to become a single state with England, becoming the United Kingdom of Great Britain. After the Act of Union 1707 the Parliament of Scotland was adjourned, and the building no longer used for its original purpose.

In the years that followed, Scotland suffered politically and economically and the people were unhappy. The Jacobites won sympathy because they were seen as defenders of Scottish liberties and pledged to repeal the Union and restore Scotland's parliament. The first Jacobite Rebellion in 1715 saw 16,000 men – two thirds of them Highlanders – join forces against the government. Afterwards the Government army built roads and barracks from Edinburgh up to the Highlands to prevent another rebellion. This is why Black Jack Randall is stationed in Scotland, and how Claire comes to meet him when she first travels through the

stones.

When Bonnie Prince Charlie lands in 1745, he used these new roads to his advantage. A journey that would previously have taken three months now takes just six weeks, enabling him to speedily gather the clans.

In Outlander, we see the Jacobite rebellion splitting families. Colum MacKenzie rules the clan with caution, remembering the 1715 defeat, where a lot of his countrymen died, leaving their starving wives and children to work the fields. Dougal, the muscle of the family, openly supports Charles's campaign, and uses Jamie's lashed back (inflicted by Black Jack Randall) to help collect rents from the villagers to support a second Jacobite rising.

These days, Parliament Hall is part of the Court of Sessions complex and is used by lawyers and their clients as a meeting place. It's open to the public (a fact not widely publicised) and is beautifully restored with an oak-beamed ceiling and grand stained glass window. Inside are many important paintings, statues and busts.

The new parliament is now on the Canongate stretch of the Royal Mile – it's a gleaming, award-winning post-modern building. You can't miss it!

4. PISSING PONY

The statue of the horse outside Parliament Hall would have been there in Jamie and Claire's time. The oldest statue in Edinburgh, it was built in 1685 and depicts Charles II (not the Bonnie Prince – he was Charles III) as a Roman emperor. The problem was, it was made of lead and corroded in the rain. Holes appeared, and when the casing filled with water in the

1690s, an anatomical hole was drilled in the bottom of the horse to let it out. From that day forwards, whenever it rained it became the 'pissing pony'.

5. LOTHIAN CHAMBERS

In Outlander S2, when Claire makes the astonishing discovery that Jamie didn't die at Culloden, she visits the National Archives in Edinburgh with Roger and Brianna. Here, they search through ships' manifests looking for his name, believing him to have been transported to the colonies. On screen, the exterior of the National Archives is a building called Lothian Chambers, which was built in 1818 and based on the design of the Acropolis. The building is now the French Embassy.

Lothian Chambers doubles as the exterior of the National Archives

Kim Traynor, geography.org.uk/p/2166061

The real National Archives, renamed the National Register of Scotland (NRS), is on 02 Princes Street. The Historical Search Room is on the first floor, so if you want to follow in Claire's footsteps and look up a Scottish ancestor of historical figure, here's the place to get started.

6. THE SIGNET LIBRARY

This lavish Georgian building on Parliament Square provided the perfect set for the Jamaica ball in Outlander S3, and it doesn't look too different in real life! It's sometimes referred to as the 'Colonnades at the Signet' because of the rows of columns outside the building. The downstairs restaurant, the Colonnades, serves lunch and afternoon teas and is used for receptions and private parties, whilst upstairs is a ballroom.

The Signet Library is also home to a prestigious body of lawyers – the WS Society. Dating back to the 15th century, these were 'Writers to Her Majesty's Signet' – officers authorised to produce royal manuscripts with the King of Scotland's seal, the 'Signet'. The classical building is Grade A listed, and was completed in 1822 for the WS Society in time for King George IV's visit to Edinburgh.

7. THE OLD TOLBOOTH

There are so many impressive buildings in Edinburgh that you're unlikely to be looking down. However, if you do happen to scan the pavements, you might have noticed the brass cobbles. Placed in the middle of Parliament Square, opposite St Giles, these mark the place where the Old Tolbooth once stood.

The 15th century building was the administrative centre of Edinburgh, a prison and site of public execution. It was demolished in 1817 and featured a year later in Sir Walter Scott's novel, The Heart of Midlothian. The heart itself – a granite mosaic – marks the site of the prison entrance, and is used in the crest of the Edinburgh football team Heart of Midlothian. It's tradition to spit on the heart – not out of disdain for the team, but for good luck apparently, though some say it's out of disdain for the former prison.

The part that Outlander fans will be interested in is the Old Tolbooth's role as a jail. In the book Dragonfly in Amber, this is a dark, dirty, rat-infested place where Jamie's Lallybroch men were locked up after they were caught deserting Charles Stuart's army. It's also where Jack Randall planned to send

Ali Wood

The Heart of Midlothian marks the entrance to the Old Tolbooth

Did you know?

Daniel Defoe was sent to Edinburgh to spy for the Crown in 1706. He believed the Union would be a good thing economically for Scotland and would help protect Protestant England against threats from the Continent. He enjoyed his time networking in the coffee houses, and saw much of Edinburgh life. As a member of the Society for the Reformation of Manners, Defoe patrolled the streets rooting out lewd and criminal behaviour – just the sort of experience he needed to later create the character Moll Flanders!

Claire after he captured her trying to escape to Craigh na Dun.

'The Tolbooth prisoners couldn't get out but there was nothing barring visitors who wanted to get in,' Claire says in Dragonfly in Amber. 'Fergus and I visited the prison daily, and a small amount of discriminating bribery allowed me to pass food and medicine to the men from Lalllybroch.'

The Old Tolbooth was eventually demolished to widen the Royal Mile so coaches could go up and down.

- **Walk from Parliament Square to Advocate's Close**

8. ADVOCATE'S CLOSE

Edinburgh's old town is famous for its wynds and closes; small alleyways and courtyards that lead off the Royal Mile. There are over 80 in total, with the most wonderful names – such as

An engraving of the Old Toll Booth, based on an 18th century painting

Fleshmarket Close and Marlin's Wynd – so-called because of a memorable resident, or a trade plied on the street.

Claire stays in a wynd above the Canongate whilst Jamie and his uncles ride to Stirling.

'It was a small, cold, cramped room, but I wasn't in it much.' She says. Carrubber's Close, a real street at the bottom of the Royal Mile, also features in the Outlander books. It's here that the Reverend Campbell and his sister Margaret stay at Henderson's Lodging House.

The rest of Diana Gabaldon's street names are fictional. 'Ladywalk Wynd' – where Alexander Randall keeps a room – doesn't exist, but there is a street called Lady Stair's Close, which is where the writer's museum is today (featuring the

Edinburgh Castle and the Nor Loch. John Slezer, Theatrum Scotiae

lives of Sir Walter Scott, Robert Louis Stevenson and Robert Burns).

Take a stroll down Advocate's Close to get an idea of the Edinburgh Jamie and Claire lived in. Look at number 4. The lintel dates the house back to 1590, and the initials refer to the young married couple for whom it was built. The blessing is in Latin and designed to protect them. To further ward off evil, it was customary to embed oyster shells in the wall. Can you see the shiny white edge between the stones? Back then, oysters were a staple diet of the poor. For the equivalent of 10p you could buy 130.

At the bottom of the steep alleyway is Princess Street Gardens. In Jamie and Claire's time this would have been a lake, the Nor Loch. Originally a marsh, it was flooded in 1460 by King James III in order to strengthen the castle's defences. As the Old Town became more crowded during the Middle Ages the Nor Loch was polluted with sewage and household waste thrown down the hillside. Notwithstanding, a specialty on the menu at Edinburgh's taverns was Nor Loch eel-pie!

Because of the steep ridge and the loch, the Old Town couldn't expand outwards, so instead people built upwards. The loch was filled in and replaced with gardens in the 1820s.

The apartments off the Royal Mile are up to 10 storeys high, whilst those at the bottom of Advocate Close are 14 storeys. Those alleyways that were shut at night were called 'closes' because the gates were closed to protect the inhabitants from criminals and drunkards. Wynds, on the other hand, were left open.

Those who went to court at Holyrood Palace lived in the Canongate, where they had enclosures, or gardens, at the back of their houses, whilst those in the upper Royal Mile lived in crowded, unsanitary conditions, with no running water and just a bucket in the corner of the room for a toilet. As you can imagine, a family of 10 would fill the bucket frequently. Rather than carry it to the bottom of the stairs, the women would simply throw it out of the window. There was nowhere to hide! The waste could be inches thick, and would pour down into the Nor Loch.

Back then people believed disease was spread by smells, so it was common to wear a pomander – a perfumed metal ball – around your neck. On your feet would be a pair of 'patents', a kind of platform heel that attached to the shoe so you could walk above the filth. In their very basic form, these were planks of wood, though nicely dressed ladies would wear more

Did you know ?

The medieval Scots term 'gardyloo' was used to warn people you were about to throw your slops out of the window. It comes from the French term 'garde à l'eau' meaning 'beware of the water'. In the 14th century young Scottish men went to Paris for their military education. They heard the wives shouting this before they emptied their chamberpots, and found it a useful expression to bring home. However, with a Scottish accent it became 'gardyloo.'

decorative pairs. Those with money, of course, would travel in a sedan chair, usually carried by Highlanders forced out by the Clearances.

When Claire visits Alexander Randall, Black Jack Randall's dying brother, she says his house was not quite a slum but the next thing to it.

'I stepped gingerly aside to avoid a substantial puddle of filth left by the emptying of chamberpots from windows overhead, awaiting removal by the next hard rain.'

In 1749, the Nastiness Act was introduced allowing people to empty their chamberpots only between the hours of 10pm and 7am. The act still exists today; it was never repealed... so if you're walking in the wynds after dark be sure to take an umbrella!

- **Walk from Advocate Close to Anchor Close**

9. ANCHOR CLOSE

In Outlander, Jamie becomes a printer under the alias of
Alexander Malcolm. It's possible that Diana Gabaldon was
inspired by an 18th century printer named William Smellie,
who lived here in Anchor Close. Smellie (1740–1795) produced
the first edition of Encyclopaedia Britannica and also edited a
weekly paper called the Scot's Journal. To pick up work he'd
frequent the taverns where all the intellectuals, poets and
philosophers met, including the poet Robert Burns. Smellie
printed the Edinburgh editions of Burns's poems and the pair
became good friends. Burns spent many an evening correcting
his proofs on a stool in Smellie's untidy office.

It was the time of the Enlightenment: ideas were being
generated faster than they could be circulated, and the city was
building a new town and university to the south. To become a

Tweedale Court is used for the market scenes in Outlander S3

VisitScotland/Kenny Lam

printer in such a time – Jamie Fraser's time – was a very smart move, and print shops were popping up everywhere.

Robert Burns, unknowingly, plays an important role in Outlander! It's a line from his poem written in 1786 that catches Roger MacKenzie's attention. 'Freedom an' whisky gang thegither!' exclaims Roger. 'I found him. Only someone with knowledge of the future could have quoted lines that hadn't been written yet. Have a look at the printer's name: Alexander Malcolm.'

- **Walk from Anchor Close to Tweeddale Court**

10. TWEEDDALE COURT, EDINBURGH

Tweeddale Court is a key location in Outlander. This beautiful street appears as a market place, with pheasants hanging from hooks, pigs, herbs and baked goods for sale in stalls. It's here that Fergus, now a grown man, spots Claire and hugs her. 'My lady,' he gasps. 'You've returned. It's a miracle.' Behind him is Tweedale House, which was built in 1576 for the Marquess of Tweeddale, a senior adviser to King Charles II. English author Daniel Defoe stayed in Edinburgh in the beginning of the 18th century. He wrote that: 'the Marquess of Tweeddale has a good city house, with a plantation of lime trees behind it instead of a garden.'

- **Walk to the World's End Pub**

11. THE WORLD'S END PUB

Need a rest after all that walking? This traditional pub is the perfect place to refuel. The World's End makes an appearance in the third Outlander book, Voyager, and is mentioned in series 3 (though the actual pub is a set). It's here that drunken Mr Willoughby gets himself in trouble and has to be rescued by Jamie. The name 'World's End' is meaningful. Opposite the pub were the gates to Edinburgh and – for most of the population – the end of their world. These people would have lived and died within the city walls, too poor to pay the toll to re-enter their own city.

The walls were built following the 1513 battle of Flodden between England and Scotland, during which James IV of Scotland was killed. The walls no longer exist, but the brass cobbles in the pavement mark where the gates would have

Opposite the World's End pub were the gates to Edinburgh

been when Bonnie Prince Charlie arrived with 3,000 men, and took Edinburgh without bloodshed.

- **Walk from the pub to Bakehouse Close**

12. BAKEHOUSE CLOSE

At last... the location you've been waiting for! Bakehouse Close doubles as Carfax Close, home to Jamie's print shop where he's reunited with Claire after 20 years of separation. This enchanting close is one of the best-preserved examples of Old Edinburgh, and the archway dates back to 1570.

The stone staircase that leads up to the timber-framed entrance was used as the exterior of A. Malcolm, printer. The building opposite plays a key role, too. Remember that Jamie

Ali Wood

Bakehouse Close is where you'll find Jamie's print shop

lives in a brothel? Well on screen you see him come out of the front door, walk down the street and round the corner to arrive at the print shop. Yet in actual fact the building used for the brothel is straight across the street.

Now the respectable HQ for Edinburgh World Heritage (with the ground floor belonging to the Museum of Edinburgh) Acheson House has a colourful history to rival the steamiest scenes in Outlander. It was built in 1633 as a grand house for newly weds Margaret Hamilton and Archibold Acheson. However, from the late 1700s until shortly before the Second World War the house became a truly disreputable brothel known as The Cock and Trumpet, after the Acheson family crest.

It's likely the brothel employed some of the girls listed in a

Acheson House was once a brothel

Ali Wood

book called Ranger's Impartial List Of Ladies Of Pleasure. Published in 1775 this offers an eye-opening description of Edinburgh's most popular prostitutes – from Betty Clark, 21, whose sulky temper can 'sometimes cool the keeneth desire' to Mrs, alias, Lady Agnew, 50, 'a drunken bundle of iniquity'!

Pop into the Museum of Edinburgh to learn more about the city's history and Jacobite past. The staff here are happy to chat about Outlander filming. Entrance at Huntly House, 142 Canongate. Open daily 10-5pm, free, www.edinburghmuseums.org.uk

- **Walk from Bakehouse Close to White Horse Close**

13. WHITE HORSE CLOSE

Prior to the release of Season 3, locals were convinced that White Horse Close would make an appearance in Outlander. Named after the white stallion belonging to Mary Queen of Scots, this was where the coach station would have been at the time Claire returned to Edinburgh. However, on screen, Claire steps out from her carriage straight into a puddle on the Royal Mile. There were a stables and a tavern known as the White Horse Inn, where Jacobite soldiers would have drank ale whilst planning the next step of the rebellion.

- **Walk to the Palace of Holyroodhouse**

14. THE PALACE OF HOLYROODHOUSE

The final stop on the Outlander walking tour is by no means the least important. Arguably, it's the most important. The Palace of Holyroodhouse, the Queen's official residence in Scotland, is where Bonnie Prince Charlie established court. Had he not, there might not have been a battle at Culloden or a story for Diana Gabaldon! In the Outlander novels Claire and Jamie visit the prince here and beg him to abandon his cause, knowing that it's hopeless.

Holyrood is a beautiful house – well worth a day's visit – and has been connected with royalty for centuries. Each year, around the end of June, the Queen and Duke of Edinburgh stay here and take part in official engagements.

You can explore the public areas and the State Apartments,

VisitScotland/Kenny Lam

Above: The Palace of Holyroodhouse
Left: Whitehorse Close

including the Throne Room and the Morning Drawing Room, as well as Mary, Queen of Scots' Chambers, where she stayed after her return from France in 1561.

Look out for the Great Gallery where Bonnie Prince Charlie held a ball, the bed where he slept and the portraits of him and his brother Henry Benedict Stuart.

In Dragonfly in Amber, Claire spends much of her time walking the grounds of Holyrood and the surrounding district, the Canongate, when flu descends on Charles Stuart and his followers.

Note, as the palace is a royal residence it can close at short notice so check the website before arrival. Open Nov to Mar: 930-430pm, Apr to Oct: 930-6pm, adults: £15.00, children 6-16: £8.70, family of 2 x adults, 3 x U17: £38.70, Canongate, rct.uk.

SCENE SPOTTER

This walking tour of Edinburgh's old town is just a glimpse of what's out there for Outlander fans! Turn to chapter 4 for some must-see locations elsewhere in the city and surrounding countryside. Meanwhile, the table below summarises the key scenes from the Outlander TV series and books.

Visit	Outlander scenes
Lothian Chambers	S2: The exterior of the National Archives
Signet Library	S3: Setting for the Jamaica ball
Bakehouse Close	S3: Carfax Close, where Jamie has a print shop

Visit	Outlander scenes
World's End Pub	Mentioned in the book Voyager
Tweedale Court	S3: Marketplace
Summerhall	S3: Lecture theatre where Claire meets Joe Abernathy
Lothian Chambers	S2: Exterior of the National Archives
Flotterstone	S1: Where Jamie is ambushed by the Redcoats
Newhailes House	S4: Where Jamie discusses land grants with Governor Tryon
Prestonpans	S2: Real-life site of the battle of Prestonpans
Preston Mill (NTS)	S1: Mill at Lallybroch and court anteroom where Geillis and Claire attend witchcraft hearing
Glencorse Old Kirk	S1: Where Jamie and Claire get married
Gosford House	S2: Stable building in the Palace of Versailles, S3: Helwater and Ellesmeere
Arniston House	S4: House in Wilmington where Claire performs surgery on Edward Fanning
Craigmillar Castle	S3: Ardsmuir Prison where Jamie is imprisoned with other Highland Jacobites
Hopetoun House	S1: Duke of Sandringham's Scottish residence, duel scene, S2: Bedroom in Jamie and Claire's Parisian apartment, Parisian streets, Mary's bedroom in Uncle Silas's house, S3: stable and riding scenes at Helwater
Midhope Castle	S1: Lallybroch exterior, S2: Cave where Jamie hides, woods where Fergus is attacked, dovecote where boys find pistol
Abercorn church	S4: Where Brianna visits Frank's grave

Chapter 4
Further afield

Now you know Edinburgh's Old Town, it's time to explore the venues on the fringe of the city and within half an hour's drive – from Lallybroch to Prestonpans, a castle, a mill and some fabulous stately homes!

SUMMERHALL

Just a 20-minute walk south of the old town is the arts venue, Summerhall, which used to be the University of Edinburgh's veterinary school. It's here in S3 that Claire meets Joe Abernathy in the anatomy lecture theatre. Edinburgh's vibrant arts scene is a must for any visitor, so why not combine your Outlander tour with some cutting-edge theatre, a ceilidh or even a gig in the old Dissection Room? It even has its own microbrewery and distillery! Reception and box office open 9-6 daily, cafe and bar open 7 days, 1 Summerhall, Edinburgh EH9 1PL, www.summerhall.co.uk.

- **Distance from old town: 1 mile/ 20-min walk**

Left: Summerhall, where Claire meets Joe Abernathy

CRAIGMILLAR CASTLE

Edinburgh's 'other castle', Craigmillar Castle appears as Ardsmuir Prison where Jamie is imprisoned with other Highland Jacobites. A mile outside the city walls, this medieval ruin once provided refuge for Mary Queen of Scots. Open Apr to Sep: 930-540pm, Oct to Mar 10-4pm, adults £6, children 5-15 £3.60, conc £4.80. EH16 4SY, www.historicenvironment. scot

- **Distance from Edinburgh: 3 miles/ 10-min drive**

FLOTTERSTONE

Flotterstone, one of the show's very first locations, is near Penicuik in the Pentland Hills Regional Park. Described by producer Ron Moore as 'the perfect place for an ambush', it's here that Jamie is shot by the Redcoats in S1. There's an information point past the Flotterstone Inn, off the A702. Here, you can pick up leaflets about the Pentland Hills, and refuel at the Pentland Hills Café Express. The Glencorse View circular walk (marked by a heron on the trail signs) is a gentle 2.7-mile footpath which leads you past the infamous ambush spot, located in a wooded area just before Glencorse Waterfall. Parking £2 donation. See www.pentlandhills.org for more info on the regional park.

- **Distance from Edinburgh: 9.5 miles/ 20-min drive**

National Trust for Scotland

Newhailies House has been undergoing conservation work

NEWHAILIES HOUSE

This elegant 17th century Palladian House in Musselburgh
appears in S4. It's here that Jamie sits down with Governor
Tryon to discuss land grants. The house, which played a
prominent role in the Scottish Enlightenment, is undergoing
serious conservation right now due to an invasion of clothes
moths! It's closed to the public for the season but you can still
visit the grounds and new Weehailes Playpark. Take the no.
30 bus to Newhailes Roundabout, or the train from Edinburgh
Waverley to Musselburgh. From here it's a 5-minute walk.
Newhailes, Musselburgh EH21 6RY, www.nts.org.uk/visit/places/
newhailes

- **Distance from Edinburgh: 9.5 miles/ 20-min drive**

PRESTONPANS

This battlesite is famous both in Scottish history and Outlander. On 21 September 1745 it was here that Jacobite forces led by the exiled Bonnie Prince Charlie defeated the government army in less than 30 minutes. It was the first significant event of the Jacobite '45 rebellion and a dramatic Jacobite victory. Though filming took place in the studio and Muiravonside country park, the production unit very carefully recreated the skyline and topography of Prestonpans. 'We're going to send the English to hell,' says Angus, memorably in episode 10, and they do, but not before he takes a fatal cannonblast wound! You can walk around the battlefields, where there are information boards, and climb the viewing platform. Battlefield Viewpoint, Prestonpans, EH33 1LZ

- **Distance from Edinburgh: 12 miles/ 20-min drive**

PRESTON MILL

Who can forget the famous mill pond scene at Lallybroch, where Jamie dives into the water to escape the Redcoats? Star of the show (aside from a dripping Jamie) was Preston Mill in East Linton. Over 150 cast and crewmembers turned up for 10 days of filming in the summer of 2014. To convincingly transform the mill into part of an 18th century estate, they had to remove fencing, signage, and gates and draft in several trees and bushes to cleverly obscure the nearby roads and houses.

The mill also stars as the court ante-room where Geillis and

VisitScotland

National Trust for Scotland

Above: Prestonpans, the site of a dramatic Jacobite victory
Below: Preston Mill was used for the mill at Lallybroch

Claire are questioned over witchcraft charges. Take a tour of the quirky meal mill, which was operational until 1959, then cross the river to Phantassie Doocot (how could you NOT visit a place called that!). Look out for otters and kingfishers en-route. The dovecote ('doocotk' is Scots) was built in the 16th century to house 500 pigeons.

Mill open May to Sep, Thu to Mon, 1230-5pm – also open on Easter Weekend (10-13 Apr 2020). Guided tours only. Last tour at 415pm. Adult £6.50, 1-adult family £11.50, family £16.50, conc £5. EH40 3DS, www.nts.org.uk/Visit/Preston-Mill.

- **Distance from Edinburgh: 24 miles/ 35-min drive**

GLENCORSE OLD KIRK

This church in the grounds of Glencorse House is where Claire and Jamie tie the knot. The house is a private family residence, open only for weddings and functions. However, if you want to pre-arrange a private tour of the kirk (Scottish word for church!), contact the owners at info@glencorsehouse.com. EH26 ONZ, glencorsehouse.co.uk

- **Distance from Edinburgh: 8 miles/ 20-min drive**

GOSFORD HOUSE

Gosford House and estate featured in both S2 and S3. The grounds and backdrop of the house were used as the luxurious

Gosford House

Gosford Housed was used in the Versailles and Helwater scenes

stable in Versailles in S2, and in S3 the house was used for the Helwater Estate, with the Robert Adam stables doubling as the stables where Jamie lived whilst working as a groom. The south wing's stunning Marble Hall was used as the interior of the Earl of Ellesmere's home.

This elegant neoclassical house is well worth a visit, though note that house and grounds tours take place on specific days only (1.5 hours), so check the website for details, call 01875 870808 or email caroline@gosfordhouse.co.uk. Private tours are also available. EH32 OPX, http://www.gosfordhouse.co.uk.

- **Distance from Edinburgh: 16 miles/ 30-min drive**

ARNISTON HOUSE

Arniston House doubles as the theatre in Wilmington where Claire's medical skills are called upon in S4, episode 8.

It's here that Governor Tryon introduces Claire and Jamie to high society, including his right-hand man Mr Fanning, and – much to Claire's delight – George and Martha Washington. Shortly after the dreadful play begins, Jamie 'accidentally' elbows Mr Fanning in the abdomen to create a diversion. Whilst Claire performs emergency surgery on Mr Fanning's hernia, Jamie nips away to warn Murtagh of the ambush.

The scene of the play itself was filmed at St Andrews in the Square, Glasgow. However, the horse and carriage approach, theatre lobby and surgery scenes – as well as the exchange between Jamie and the Washingtons – were filmed at Arniston House.

The present owner of Arniston, Mrs Althea Dundas-Bekker, inherited the home in 1970 at the age of 30, something she describes as 'bitter sweet'.

'Bitter because it involved the premature deaths of close members of my family,' she says. 'Sweet because of what Arniston is'.

A fond favourite of Sir Walter Scott, this 6,000-acre estate has more than four centuries of family history and has played an important role in Scottish and World historical events.

A popular wedding venue with holiday cottages on site, Arniston also hosts events such as fireworks and Shakespeare performances. You can book a special Outlander location tour for groups of 10-20. The guided tour includes lunch, a short video and Q&A. Check out the website for more details. The grounds are free to explore on open days.

May and June: grounds open Tues & Weds 12-5pm with

guided tours at 2pm & 330pm; Jul to mid-Sep: grounds open Tues, Weds & Sun from 12-5pm with guided tours at 2pm & 330pm. Tickets available online or at the door ranging from £3-17. Private tour groups welcome year round, www.arnistonhouse.com

• **Distance from Edinburgh: 12 miles/ 30-min drive**

HOPETOUN HOUSE

A 30-minute drive outside of Edinburgh, this 17th century stately home doubles as the home of the Duke of Sandringham. One of the finest examples of Scotland's grand architecture, it's so huge its clock towers had to be digitally

Ali Wood

The west facade of Hopetoun House where the duel was filmed

chopped off for TV. As fans will know, it's pretty impressive on-screen, but in real life it's, well... flabbergasting. Upstairs you'll find the spare room in Jamie and Claire's Parisian apartment, and downstairs the drawing room where the duke receives Claire.

Outside, the cobbled streets stand in for the Parisian streets where Claire and Mary are attacked, and the stables and grounds were used for scenes at Helwater, including those with Geneva and Willie. In S1, the beauitful lawn outside the west facade is where the duel was filmed between Jamie and the head of the McDonald clan.

Open daily Apr to Sep: 1030-5pm, adults £10.50, children £5.50, family (2+2) £28, conc £5.50, hopetoun.co.uk.

- **Distance from Edinburgh: 15 miles/ 30-min drive**

Ali Wood

The bedroom appeared in Claire and Jamie's Parisian apartment

Ali Wood

The Red Drawing Room at Hopetoun House

MIDHOPE CASTLE

Don't leave Hopetoun without first buying a permit for
Midhope Castle from the gift shop. The building provides the
exterior for Jamie's family home Lallybroch. Be warned, it's
not the jolly Fraser farm you find in Outlander, but a lonely
ruin with 'Danger keep out' signs tacked to Perspex covered
windows. It's atmospheric all the same, and two centuries ago
housed 10 families of estate workers, including gamekeepers,
foresters and carpenters. Opposite the car park are the woods
where Jamie hides in S3. The mossy outcrop by the river was
digitally remastered into his cave. EH30 9SL, hopetoun.co.uk/
access-midhope-castle, £5

• **Distance from Edinburgh: 15 miles/ 30-min drive**

ABERCORN CHURCH

Nearby, Abercorn church is where Brianna is seen visiting Frank's grave in S4. Whilst sadly you won't be able to pay your respects to Frank, you can take a look at the fine collection of old gravestones. Many date back to the 1600s, before widespread literacy, so are illustrated with skulls and bones (emblems of mortality), and angels, cherubs or doves (immortality). The symbols also show the trade of the buried person, so for example, a horseshoe means a blacksmith, and a rolling pin a baker. Abercorn EH30 9SL.

- **Distance from Edinburgh: 15 miles/ 30-min drive**

National Trust for Scotland

When you've explored Edinburgh it's time to head north to Glen Coe

NOW SEE SCOTLAND!

So that's the end of your tour. How did you get on? I'd love to know: email me at tvtraveller@outlook.com and don't forget to leave a review on Amazon! You can also join my mailing list at www.trtraveller.co.uk and I'll keep you updated on other film, book and TV-themed tours.

Happy travels,

   Ali

VisitScotland

The remote Cairngorms are where Claire and Jamie go riding

GET THE MAP

The Scottish tourist board, VisitScotland, recently created its biggest set-jetting map of Outlander to date. You can collect a map from the iCentre in Edinburgh, 3 Princes Street. Or for more information, call +44 (0)131 473 3868, www.visitscotland.com.

GET THE BOOK

Don't miss this packed guide to Scottish Outlander locations. From Edinburgh to Inverness, Skye and Glasgow, *Scotland an Outlander Tour* contains OVER 80 meticulously researched places, three self-drive itineraries, and behind-the-scenes interviews with location managers. Even non-fans will love these stunning castles, vast lochs and remote Highland escapes! Find it on Amazon or email tvtraveller@outlook.com. Stay up-to-date by subscribing to the TV Traveller mailing list at www.tvtraveller.co.uk.

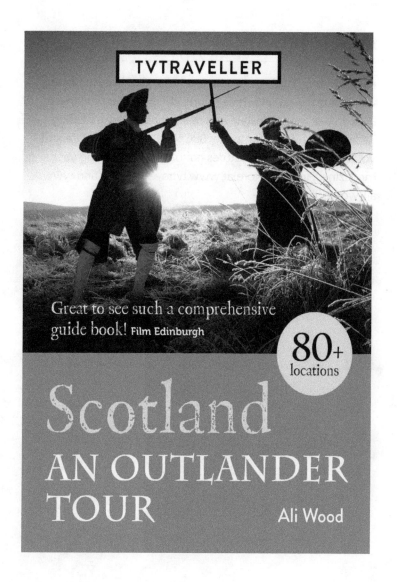

TVTRAVELLER

Great to see such a comprehensive guide book! Film Edinburgh

80+
locations

Scotland
AN OUTLANDER
TOUR
Ali Wood

ABOUT THE AUTHOR

Ali Wood is a British magazine journalist. She lives in Dorset with her husband and three young children. Her work has appeared in many lifestyle and travel magazines, including Radio Times, BBC Countryfile, BBC Wildlife, Country Life and Voyage. She's also the features editor of a best-selling yachting magazine. Find out more at www.tvtraveller.co.uk and www. ali-wood.com

CPSIA information can be obtained
at www.ICGtesting.com
Printed in the USA
BVHW011403060420
576985BV00004B/160

9 781916 263109